The Putter Principle

The Putter Principle

Golf's Greatest Legends Discuss
The Ultimate Stroke

Compiled and Edited by Criswell Freeman

WALNUT GROVE PRESS
Nashville, TN 37205

ISBN 1-887655-39-5

The ideas expressed in this book are not, in all cases, exact quotations, as some have been edited for clarity and brevity. In all cases, the author has attempted to maintain the speaker's original intent. In some cases, material for this book was obtained from secondary sources, primarily print media. While every effort was made to ensure the accuracy of these sources, the accuracy cannot be guaranteed. For additions, deletions, corrections or clarifications in future editions of this text, please write WALNUT GROVE PRESS.

Printed in the United States of America
Cover Design by Mary Mazer
Typesetting & Page Layout by Sue Gerdes
Editor for Walnut Grove Press: Alan Ross
1 2 3 4 5 6 7 8 9 10 • 97 98 99 00 01

ACKNOWLEDGMENTS
The author gratefully acknowledges the helpful support of Angela Beasley, Dick and Mary Freeman, and Mary Susan Freeman.

For Jim Harper

Thanks for the Lessons

Table of Contents

Introduction

Perhaps more than any other activity in sports, putting is a test of mind over matter. As Mickey Wright correctly observed, "Putting is a psychology, not a system." This book examines the mysterious art of putting through the words of golf's greatest teachers and practitioners.

It goes without saying that the golfer who wishes to lower his handicap must first improve his putting skills. Fully half the game is played on or around the greens. But putting is a curious combination of physical and mental activities; as such, it is not always amenable to an easy cure. On the pages that follow, we examine the psychology and physiology of golf's ultimate stroke. As you improve your putting skills, you'll inevitably learn a lesson or two about life.

Bobby Locke once observed, "You can tell a good putt by the noise it makes." Hopefully, this book will help you compose the most beautiful music in golf: the sound of a well-hit putt.

1

The Ultimate Stroke

In life, it's the little things that make all the difference. And so it is in golf. Putting, the shortest shot on the links, is also the most important.

Champagne Tony Lema wrote, "The object of this game is to put the ball into a hole which has a diameter of 4¼ inches. The rest is prologue, just a cross-country wild goose chase in search of a climax. The ultimate stroke, the one that ends all discussion, is the putt."

On the pages that follow, some of history's foremost players discuss the ultimate stroke: putting. It's the little big shot of golf.

A tap-in of half an inch counts the same as a drive of 280 yards.

Arnold Palmer

Three shots and one putt count four. I always understood that.

Walter Hagen

Putting is more than half the game.

Arnold Palmer

Statistically, putting is 68 percent
of the game of golf.

Gary McCord

No one has yet won a tournament by hitting
the most fairways or greens in regulation.

Billy Casper

You have to be a good putter to be a good
golfer, but you don't necessarily have to be a
good golfer to be a good putter.

Tony Lema

You'll never be a complete golfer
until you become a good putter.

Curtis Strange

The man who can putt is a match
for anyone.

Willie Park, Jr.

You live by the putter, and you die
by the putter.

Old Golf Saying

Neglect of the putting skills verges
on the criminal.

Ian Woosnam

Putting is an inexact science.

Gary Player

Putting is the one part of the game
with the fewest existing guidelines.

Arnold Palmer

Putting is mystical and comes and goes
like the tide.

Gary McCord

There is no similarity between golf and putting; they are two different games — one played in the air, and the other on the ground.

Ben Hogan

You work all your life to perfect a repeating swing that will get you to the greens, and then you have to try to do something that is totally unrelated. There shouldn't be any cups, just flag sticks. And then the man who hits the most fairways and greens and gets closest to the pins would be the tournament winner.

Ben Hogan

When you struggle with the putter, it gets
to the rest of your game.

Ben Crenshaw

Consistent skill around the greens is the
biggest asset a golfer can have.

Gay Brewer

To think in terms of your longest, straightest
tee shot counting exactly the same as
a six-inch putt puts into perspective
the importance of putting.

David Leadbetter

Drive for show, putt for dough.

Old Golf Saying

Being a big hitter
isn't that important.
The woods are
full of them.

Jim Thorpe

How good you become
at putting depends upon
how bad you want to.
Anybody can become
a good putter.

Gay Brewer

2

The Putter Principle

Almost one hundred years ago, Walter J. Travis observed, "Putting is largely mental, and on this account becomes so difficult." Things haven't changed much since then.

Given the paramount importance of sound putting psychology, I submit the following declaration of golfing independence which I have chosen to name "The Putter Principle": *The art of sound putting is a unique blend of physical skill and mental attitude. Once a few mechanical principles are learned through repetition, successful putting becomes an exercise in judgment and inner calm. Because putting is primarily psychological, skills can be improved most profoundly through the use of proper mental preparation and discipline.*

Gary Player once wrote, "We create success on the course primarily by our thoughts." Nowhere is this statement more true than on the greens. There's great comfort in Player's observation. It means that you too can become a great putter — if you put your mind to it.

The most important element of good putting is the ability to concentrate on the problem at hand.

Bobby Jones

A player's putting skill on a given day is in direct ratio to his confidence that day.

Cary Middlecoff

All negative, self-deprecating "inner chatter"
has to stop.

David Leadbetter

Putting is 90 percent mental.
If you think you can't putt, you're right.

Gay Brewer

All good putters are confident putters.

Cary Middlecoff

Aptitude starts with attitude.

Greg Norman

Belief is a great aid to underpinning confidence, and it's confidence that really matters when the crunch comes.

Ian Woosnam

Confidence tends to snowball.

Arnold Palmer

Confidence is the key to a successful putting technique.

Tony Lema

Psyche yourself up, not out.

Curtis Strange

If there's a secret to great putting,
visualization is it.

Arnold Palmer

In putting, visualization is everything.

Gary McCord

It's as simple as this: If you don't
concentrate, you're not playing your best.

Gary Player

If you concentrate on making the putt, you'll find it hard to figure out ways to miss it.

Gay Brewer

The art of putting at golf resembles that of goalkeeping at soccer, in being "a game within a game." Furthermore, both are games which enable a fellow with a certain crafty cunning to neutralize the efforts of stronger, braver men, and this in any walk of life is a source of much inward satisfaction.

Henry Longhurst

Your frame of reference must be exactly the width of the cup, not the general vicinity.

Jack Nicklaus

To me, positive thinking is part of concentration.

Gary Player

Make up your mind what you are going to do, then go ahead and do it.

Bobby Locke

When you lip out several putts in a row,
you should never think that means that
you're putting well and that "your share" are
about to start falling. The difference between
"in" and "almost" is all in your head.

Jack Nicklaus

Some fellows are afraid that if they talk
about their putting the touch will go away.
So they think the best thing is to moan
about it even when they're putting good.

Don January

Golf is indeed a simple game. It is the rest
of us that make it so difficult.

Henry Longhurst

Bad putting is due
more to the effect the
green has upon the player
than it has upon the
action of the ball.

Bobby Jones

Putting takes more guts than any other part
of the game because it's mostly mental.

Curtis Strange

Technique is no more than five percent
of putting. Putting is nearly all in the mind.

Bob Charles

One thing is very true. The better you putt,
the bolder you play.

Don January

The best way to build confidence is to succeed.

Lee Trevino

Don't be a negative putter.

Billy Casper

3

The Putting Stroke

U.S. Open champ Lou Graham wrote, "There is nothing, and I mean nothing, in golf that is as important as the putting stroke." Certainly no written words can take the place of competent professional advice. Nor will time spent in the library ever replace time spent on the practice green. But on the pages that follow, we consider important elements of a dependable, repeatable putting stroke. That little stroke comprises the big foundation of a solid golf game.

The putting stroke is simplest of all because it is the shortest.

Bobby Jones

Change as little as possible from one type of shot to the next. I carry this right through to the putter as well.

Ian Woosnam

In putting, the fewer moving parts there are, the simpler and more consistent your method will probably be.

David Leadbetter

Keep the stroke as simple as possible.

Gay Brewer

It is utterly impossible for any golfer to play good golf without a swing that will repeat.

Ben Hogan

Putting is the one part of the game with the fewest existing guidelines.

Arnold Palmer

There are six fundamentals of putting: grip, balance, steadiness, eyes over the line, square shoulders, and a low smooth swing.

Curtis Strange

For every putt you ever make, once the machinery is set in action, go through the same motions. No extra waggle, no extra look at the hole.

Henry Longhurst

Balance the backswing with the forward
　　swing, like a clock pendulum.

Gay Brewer

Address the putt with your eyes
　　directly over the ball.

Gary Player

In addressing the putt, the feet do not
necessarily have to be square to the line, but
　　the clubface must definitely be square.

Billy Casper

Make sure your putterhead *never* moves
　　outside your line during your stroke.

Lee Trevino

Palmer's technique of staying motionless
over a putt, solid as a statue, is envied by all.

Dan Jenkins

Head movement is a prime cause
of missed putts.

Arnold Palmer

If your head moves, the blade moves —
just enough to make you miss the putt.

Judy Rankin

Consistent putting requires that the player
keep his body steady.

Cary Middlecoff

Stay down and don't move.

Arnold Palmer

Good putters keep their body still during
the stroke.

Gary Player

Good putters don't raise their heads until
the ball is partway along the line to the cup.

Cary Middlecoff

To become a good putter, the main requisites
are to keep the head dead still and
make the putter blade go accurately
toward the chosen line.

Tommy Armour

You notice when Arnold Palmer addresses
the putt, pigeon-toed and knees pinched
together, nothing moves but the hands
and forearms. That's the secret.

Byron Nelson

Generally speaking, the wrists, when held
firmly, will take very good care of themselves.

Harry Vardon

Nothing ruins the consistency of a putting
stroke like unwanted wrist action
through impact.

David Leadbetter

We would all be better putters if we didn't
have a left wrist.

Al Geiberger

Fine putters make the blade travel
in a very flat arc.

Bobby Jones

The main thing great putters have
in common is that they bring the clubhead
into the ball square with the intended line,
they contact the ball solidly,
and they practice a lot.

Gary Player

Try to hit the ball with the clubhead
accelerating at impact.

Bob Rosburg

Keep both hands moving toward the target
through impact.

Arnold Palmer

Keep the putter low on the follow-through.
This will help you keep your head down.

Gary Player

If you can keep the blade square throughout
the stoke, then one of the variables has been
removed from the equation.

Ian Woosnam

On follow-through, I keep the clubface
square and my head down.

Bobby Locke

Let the club swing freely without arriving at
any abrupt stopping place.

Bobby Jones

Maintain acceleration by not taking
the putter back too far.

Al Geiberger

All good putters have balance.

Arnold Palmer

All good putters hit the ball solidly.

Cary Middlecoff

A firm stroke is a good stroke.

Greg Norman

Most players don't aim
as well as they imagine.

Nick Faldo

Your shot will always start out
  in the direction your clubhead is moving
      when it strikes the ball.

Jack Grout

Strike the ball from straight behind it.

Greg Norman

Every putt you will ever have in your life,
on any course, of any length, is dead straight.
On a sharp slope, the ball may roll almost in a
semicircle, but you did not make it so. All you
can do, time and time again, is to hit it dead
    straight — not necessarily, of course,
        straight at the hole.

Bobby Locke

The little waggle before a putt has a very
definite purpose: to make my stroke
as smooth and rhythmic as possible.

Billy Casper

One of the golden rules in putting is that
the length of your stroke should always
control the distance you hit the ball.

David Leadbetter

Imagine there's a second ball placed
two inches (toward the target) in front of the
real one. Now, accelerate the putterhead
smoothly through the imaginary ball,
sending it straight into the hole.

Fred Couples

If you contact the sweet spot every time, you'll be on the way to solid putting.

Lee Trevino

I don't believe in taking a lot of practice strokes and standing over the ball until my muscles tense up.

Lee Trevino

I have seen some putting styles that look like they came off a drawing board at Disney.

Tony Lema

No matter how perfectly
you stroke any putt,
there's no guarantee
it's going to drop
into the hole.

Fred Couples

Having acquired a fairly smooth and accurate stroke, the thing for me to do is forget it and swing.

Bobby Jones

4

Know Thyself

Six hundred years before the birth of Christ, the sage Lao-Tzu advised, "Knowing others is wisdom. Knowing yourself is enlightenment." Greg Norman echoed these words when he warned, "Be brutally honest in the appraisal of the state of your game."

If the state of your putting skills could stand improvement, begin with an inventory of your strengths and weaknesses. Then go take a lesson or two. And above all, don't forget to turn the page.

There is no one right way to wield the putter.

Arnold Palmer

Each of us should find a putting technique that suits us.

Greg Norman

No one should know better than you whether you can hit a certain shot or not.

Harvey Penick

I play along every year, waiting for one week, maybe two, when I can putt.

Larry Nelson

The fine art of putting is a compendium of gimmicks, psychological crutches and mental sleight of hand.

Tony Lema

Beware of change for change's sake.

Ian Woosnam

Take inventory of
your game after every
day of play.

Sam Snead

The devoted golfer is an anguished soul who has learned a lot about putting just as an avalanche victim has learned a lot about snow.

Dan Jenkins

Before trying something different, check that nothing has changed to make you putt badly.

Ian Woosnam

Know what your skills are, and trust them.

Greg Norman

Putting is a personal thing.

Ian Woosnam

Self-knowledge leads to confidence.

Greg Norman

Just get comfortable. Then stroke the putt
the best way you know how.

Billy Casper

If there's one thing I've learned, it's to play golf your way, instead of playing like somebody else.

Gary Player

There's no point in discussing putting styles. You grope around, shuffle, bend, re-shuffle, twist and writhe until you find a putting stance that feels comfortable — to you.

Tony Lema

5

Practice

In 1872, the British statesman Benjamin Disraeli observed, "The secret of success is constancy of purpose." Disraeli could have been describing the lifelong pursuit for the perfect putting stroke.

The great Billy Casper observed, "The solution to golf, if there is one, is this: Learn how to putt before anything else." Another golfing legend, Ben Hogan, was asked about his tireless work habits. He responded, "Every day you miss playing or practicing is one day longer it takes to be good."

If you're seeking a solution to the enigma of putting, consider the words of two Bens and a Billy: Keep practicing until you get it right.

If I had my early life in golf to live over, I would practice my putting twice as much as I did.

Gary Player

Practice three- and four-footers twice as much as you practice long putts.

Billy Casper

M̲r. Average Golfer spends too much time
tinkering with his long game at the expense
of the short.

Ian Woosnam

P̲ractice putting may not be the most
enjoyable golf work, but it is certainly
the most important.

Lou Graham

S̲ince no two greens are the same,
practice and judgment based on experience
will help you more than any instruction.

Doug Sanders

Putting is like wisdom, partly a natural gift
and partly accumulation of experience.

Arnold Palmer

Nobody has enough natural ability
to become a real champion. You've got to
know the fundamentals of the game
to get up there and stay up there.

Gary Player

You can't make some casual "wouldn't it be
nice" half-decision about where you'd like
to go with your game. Improvement
takes time and patience.

Sam Snead

Begin by practicing the short putts first.

Billy Casper

Routine is important in putting.

Judy Rankin

Practice until you feel you are putting well,
and then stop before you spoil your stroke.

Jack Nicklaus

Putting is something that needs
constant attention.

Ian Woosnam

The more I practice, the luckier I get.

Gary Player

The stand-out putters on the tour are the
guys who wear grooves in practice greens
and motel rugs.

Gay Brewer

Make a game out of practice.
You're still a child at heart.

Harvey Penick

Golf is a great game but a very selfish game.
It lets you get out of it only as much
as you put in.

Sam Snead

Never lose the will to improve.

Tom Watson

The only way to build realistic confidence in yourself is through practice.

Sam Snead

Practice makes pars.

Gay Brewer

6

Finding a Putter That Works

Sam Snead spoke for golfers of every generation when he said, "Of all clubs, the putter is the most fickle and difficult to find." Snead's observation is true for the vast majority of duffers and pros alike. Like Diogenes searching for an honest man, we search in vain for a thoroughly reliable putter.

For pros and weekend warriors alike, the search for the perfect putter is akin to the search for the Holy Grail. And for most of us, the search continues.

Finding the perfect
putter has been the
eternal search of all
golfing mankind.

Ian Woosnam

Your putter is the most important club
in your bag.

Harvey Penick

A new putter may work for a few rounds,
but eventually the real cause of the problem —
technique — comes back to haunt you.

Lee Trevino

Find a putter you like and stay with it
through good times and bad.

Harvey Penick

Select a putter that is easy to line up.

Billy Casper

The sweet spot is the area of the putter face
that produces the most solid impact.
Find it.

Arnold Palmer

You can't go into a shop and
buy a good golf game.

Sam Snead

Properly fitted clubs are the only part
of improved golf that anyone can buy.

Tommy Armour

With putting, success is dependent on the human head, not the putter head.

Arnold Palmer

The belief that it's the weapon not the man
has kept club pros in funds ever since
the game began.

Ian Woosnam

Choosing a putter is like selecting a wife or
girl friend. There are all types. Merely pick the
one that appeals to you in which you have
the most faith and confidence.

Eddie Merrins

It goes without saying that a player should
find a putter in which he has full confidence.

Cary Middlecoff

What kind of putter is best? The one in the most confident hands.

Bob Rosburg

During those spells when your putter quits working, resist the urge to go buy a different putter. Your old familiar putter really hasn't quit working.

Harvey Penick

Nine times out of ten, a change from one type of putter to another will effect no lasting good.

Bobby Jones

Punish your putter by hiding it in the closet if you must, but keep it. The time will come when you dig it out and find that it works again.

Harvey Penick

The feel of a long-used putter is programmed into your nervous system.

Arnold Palmer

Never get rid of a putter that feels right. Eventually it will feel right again.

Sam Snead

You can't let a putter think it's indispensable. I switch at least once a year, just to prove to old Betsy that she can be switched.

Fuzzy Zoeller

I've got 150 putters in my basement.

Charlie Owens

I'm having putting troubles. But it's not the putter, it's the puttee.

Frank Beard

7

Peaceful Putting

Putting, by its very nature, is a nerve-racking experience. But somehow the best golfers find a way to remain peaceful in the face of embarrassment, financial loss, or both. Henry Cotton, one of the finest putters of his day, advised, "The big trick in putting is in the domination of the nerves rather than in the method." No kidding.

In this chapter, we search for calm waters amid the psychological storms that accompany the act of putting a small white ball toward its proper resting place. May it rest in peace.

Good putters remain relaxed.

Henry Cotton

There's no room on the golf course
for anger or self-pity.

Greg Norman

A wise man doesn't concern himself
with things he can't control.

Calvin Peete

The best thing anyone can do as a putter is
to learn to roll with the punches. Try to take
the bitter with the sweet.

Fred Couples

The things that hurt my putting the most
when it was bad — and it was very bad
at times — was thinking too much.

Bobby Jones

Great putters concentrate on cause
rather than result.

Cary Middlecoff

Putting is mental. You must put the fear
of failure out of your mind.

Harvey Penick

Sometimes you end up missing putts mainly
because you are afraid of missing them.

Arnold Palmer

Attitude is more important on the greens
than anywhere else on the golf course.

Gay Brewer

Good putting is a state of mind.

Arnold Palmer

The best putters are the
breezy and optimistic
people. Poor putters,
by contrast, seem to be
cranky and cantankerous
characters.

Tony Lema

Pressure putting is what separates the good golfer from the *really* good golfer.

Gay Brewer

I do not think the secret of putting,
if there is a secret, is in the mechanics.

Bobby Jones

I really do believe that putting
is inspirational, not mechanical.

Jack Nicklaus

Mechanics are important, but when it gets
down to the nitty-gritty, it's heart that sets
those mechanics in motion and gets the ball
into the cup.

Curtis Strange

Try not to think too deeply about putting.

Gary McCord

By its very nature, putting is a hugely
personal matter.

David Leadbetter

The man who says his knees aren't shaking
as he stands over a this-to-win putt is lying.

Ian Woosnam

There can be a no more ludicrous sight than
that of a grown man, a captain of industry
perhaps and a pillar of his local community,
convulsively jerking a piece of ironmongery
to and fro in his efforts to hole a three-foot
putt. I refer to what Tommy Armour
once christened the "yips."

Henry Longhurst

The "yips" is that ghastly time when,
with the first movement of the putter, the
golfer blacks out, loses sight of the ball and
hasn't the remotest idea of what to do with
the putter or, occasionally, that he is holding
a putter at all.

Tommy Armour

My advice to the weekend warrior is to bang the ball boldly.

Tony Lema

The simpler the stroke, the more effective
it will be under pressure.

Billy Casper

Becoming too careful, trying to be
too precise, causes a golfer to freeze
over his putt.

Bobby Jones

In putting, anxiety creates poor tempo.

Al Geiberger

Indecision almost always leads
to deceleration.

Arnold Palmer

Miss 'em quick.

Gene Sarazen

Hit the putt before it hits you.

Bob Rosburg's Theory

My concept of putting starts
with getting comfortable.

Al Geiberger

Mental poise and equanimity account
for some 90 percent of putting success.

Tony Lema

There are many putter designs. But the main
factor in putters is the mental attitude
of the player at the end of the stick.

Bob Rosburg

I resolved never to make a putt in an important round when my breath was hurried.

Bobby Jones

Remember, a putt is a caress of the ball, not an uninhibited bash.

Ian Woosnam

During a steak of bad putting, one is tempted to tighten the grip, shorten the swing, and try to guide the ball into the hole. Resist these temptations at all costs.

Bobby Jones

To be consistently effective, you must put a certain distance between yourself and what happens to you out on the golf course.

Sam Snead

My attitude of giving it my best shot and
accepting the consequences has made me a
much better putter over the long haul.

Fred Couples

Somewhere in there, skill stops and
luck takes over.

Jerry Barber

Take it easy on yourself when you miss one.

Arnold Palmer

No man is at peace with the game of golf.

Thomas Boswell

Hit the putt as well as you can, and do not worry over the outcome to ruin the stroke.

Bobby Jones

8

To Lag or Not To Lag

Hamlet's question, "To be or not to be?" seems to pale in comparison to the golfer's continual conundrum: to lag or not to lag. On almost every hole, or so it seems, we duffers face the slings and arrows of outrageous fate, otherwise known as approach putts.

All golfers should formulate personal strategies for attacking the challenge of curling forty-footers. Otherwise, when the moment of truth arrives, as it must, we fall prey to paralyzing indecision. And three-putt.

I do not believe that any man can be so
accurate in striking a ball and precise in judgment that he can propel a golf ball over ten
yards of uneven turf with such unerring cer-
tainty that it will always find a spot
the size of a hole.

Bobby Jones

When hitting an approach putt, try to lag
the ball into an imaginary three-foot circle.

Billy Casper

In a lifetime of playing, teaching and watching
golf, I have seen very few three-putts caused
by missing a second putt that is a little short
of the hole. On the other hand, I have seen
countless three putts caused by missing a
second putt that is three or four feet
beyond the hole.

Harvey Penick

Try to make every putt that lands ten feet from the hole or closer. Hope to make every putt from ten to twenty feet. From twenty feet and beyond, try to get it close.

Gary McCord

I think it is advisable to try generally to sink putts that are within about twenty feet.

Sam Snead

On putts of thirty feet or more, be realistic: Try to get down in two.

Curtis Strange

The greedy golfer will go too near and be sucked into his own destruction.

John Low, 1902

The golfer who tries
to hole all his putts is
usually the one with
the most three-putts.

Sam Snead

The best way to get close is to try to get in.
Cary Middlecoff

If you think the game is just a matter
of getting it close and letting the law of
averages do your work for you, you'll find
a different way to miss every time.
Jack Nicklaus

A putt left short is a putt lost. Putt boldly.
Greg Norman

Let your putts die at the hole and give luck
a chance.

Harvey Penick

The putt that is struck too firmly has only
one way into the cup; dead center. But if
a dying ball touches the rim, it drops.

Bobby Jones

Your style of putting probably reflects
the style you normally play from tee to green.

Arnold Palmer

If you hit the ball a bit too hard,
  watch the way it rolls as it passes the hole.
  It's an immediate read on the return putt.
                                        Greg Norman

The best putters have the guts
    to get up there and give it a chance.
                                        Tommy Bolt

There is nothing odd about rolling
        in thirty-footers.
                                        Arnold Palmer

Good putting is the banishment of doubt.

Ian Woosnam

In golf, loss of self-control
is reflected in poor
decision-making.

Curtis Strange

9

Short Putts

Bruce Devlin once noted, "What counts most is the ability to consistently hole putts from six feet or less." Easier said than done.

The tragedy of a bungled three-footer is the tragedy of senseless loss. Once missed, that little putt looms as large on the scorecard as a booming 300-yard drive. Perhaps this explains why missed three-footers are almost impossible to forget or forgive.

If the truth be told, short putts have frightened more golfers than all the water hazards, bunkers, trees and cart paths combined. But now is the time to banish those fears forever — or at least until the next one rims out.

Missing a short putt is about the most humiliating thing in the world because you're supposed to make it.

Byron Nelson

The short putt is one of the most psychologically demanding parts of the game.

Arnold Palmer

A short putt is the least physically demanding shot in golf — and the most psychologically taxing.

Curtis Strange

I practice hitting short putts, not to hone my technique, but to hone my nerves.

Greg Norman

I can't get over the fact that I can hit two great shots covering 440 yards, and be four feet from the cup, and if I miss that little-bitty putt, it counts as much as the two great shots.

Orville Moody

There is nothing so demoralizing as missing a short putt.

Bobby Jones

If you come out of the chute leaving yourself
a lot of three and four-footers, you use up
a lot of nerve early in the round.

Sam Snead

Long second putts take a lot out of you,
even when you make 'em.

Cary Middlecoff

There is nothing in golf that bears down with
quite the pressure of having to continually
hole out putts of three and four feet.

Bobby Jones

The last thing I ever want to see on a golf
course is a nasty four-footer for par.

Paul Azinger

Putting affects the nerves more than anything.
I would actually get nauseated
over a three-footer.

Byron Nelson

There was a time when I honestly would have
rather faced a ten-foot putt that had to be
holed than one of three feet.

Bobby Jones

You rarely get the "yips" on long putts.
But on short putts you want to "peek" at the
hole. Darting, jumpy eyes are a big cause
for the "yips."

Judy Rankin

All of us tend to become a little
too tentative at times on the short ones.

Jack Nicklaus

On short putts, instead of being determined to put the ball into the hole, we too often become consumed with the fear of failing to do so.

Bobby Jones

When you're standing over a short putt, focus on the ball, not the hole.

Judy Rankin

The majority of short putts are missed by looking for imaginary slopes and hitting the ball softly, trying to "baby" it into the cup.

Tommy Armour

Putting problems arise when you try to "help" the ball into the hole.

David Leadbetter

When we try not to miss a short putt,
 our determination, if we may call it such,
  is negative.

Bobby Jones

Don't ever think about what will happen
 if you miss a putt. That's negative thinking.

Gay Brewer

I'm convinced that your subconscious can't
tell the difference between reality and dream.
You have to paint a mental picture of your
future in detail. All those six-foot putts are
made in the back of your head. You can't
do it unless you've imagined it first.

Peter Jacobsen

The key to short putts is confidence.

Curtis Strange

With a short putt, I very definitely keep
my head still and at all costs never look up
to see where the ball is going.

Nick Faldo

If you aim a shorter putt at the cup
and concentrate on striking the ball with the
sweet spot of the putter, you will make
your share.

Harvey Penick

On short putts, don't worry so much about
distance. Concentrate on aiming the
putterhead and rolling the ball straight.

Curtis Strange

Imagine a pair of hands about a foot behind
the hole, positioned so that they're encircling
the back of the cup. Determine to stroke the
ball right into the center of those hands.

Fred Couples

On putts of three feet or less, don't aim
outside the edge of the cup. Very rarely will
the ball break below the hole.

Curtis Strange

Most people three-putt not because they
misread the break, but because they didn't hit
the putt with the correct speed.

Nancy Lopez

If the greens aren't in tip-top condition,
it's easy to miss short putts by not hitting
the ball firmly enough.

Nick Faldo

The mental attitude with which we approach
a short putt has a lot to do with our success.

Bobby Jones

On the practice green, once your confidence
is rock-solid from two feet, increase it to four.

Curtis Strange

Moving your head or your eyes
on a short putt is a result of fear.

Harvey Penick

To miss a three-foot putt
seems the most useless
thing in the world.

Bobby Jones

Realize that even with the short ones, you can't make them all.

Curtis Strange

10

Reading the Green

The legendary Bobby Locke once observed, "Most putts are missed not because they are poorly hit, but because they are started on the wrong line and at the wrong speed." Thus we are introduced to the most meticulous mental exercise in golf: reading a green.

Ben Hogan correctly noted that putting is different from golf. Golf, he said, is played in the air while putting is played on the ground. Since putts remain earthbound, it's our job to scout out the terrain and give them the best chance to drop.

For the weekend duffer, reading a green is akin to reading tea leaves, only with instant feedback. But to the seasoned veteran, the green becomes an open book. And now for a few reading lessons.

Seeing the line is a curious thing and I am
free to confess I do not well understand it.
Bobby Jones

Green reading is an art, not a science.
Judy Rankin

Good green reading comes with experience.
Greg Norman

Reading a putt is a "marriage" of the
contours of the ground and the speed
of the putt.
Fred Couples

Putting doesn't start when you're standing over the ball. I start putting as soon as I can see the ball and the cup.

Gay Brewer

Feel the green with your feet as you walk.

Patty Sheehan

The successful putter considers all details when picking the line for his putt.

Gary Player

Four main conditions need to be observed: slope, green texture, grain and wind. The main variable is slope.

Arnold Palmer

Cultivate the habit of setting up
a procedure for sizing up your putt.

Arnold Palmer

Study putts from behind the ball to judge
the break, and then from the low side
of the hole to see if the putt is either
uphill or downhill.

Ken Venturi

We should concern ourselves mainly
with general contours of a slope rather than
every little hop or roll the ball might take.

Bobby Jones

Reading a putt is mainly an exercise
in determining speed.

Gay Brewer

Your first impression
of a putt is probably
the correct one.

Patty Sheehan

Serious golfers well understand how
important it is to know all about grass.

Arnold Palmer

The ball turns in the direction of the grain.

Gary Player

Look into the hole. Grass lying across
the rim of the cup will reveal the direction
of any grain.

Arnold Palmer

While wet greens will naturally slow down
the ball, there will also be less break
than normal.

Fred Couples

Weekend golfers underplay breaking putts
and tour pros overplay them.

Tom Watson

Very few golfers take any wind into sufficient consideration when putting.

James Braid

Plumb-bobbing will not necessarily tell you which way a putt will break, but it *will* tell you in which direction the ground you're standing on slopes.

Curtis Strange

Plumb-bobbing has its place as a guide in specific situations, but the essence of golf is human judgment.

Arnold Palmer

Putts always run toward nearby water.

Sam Snead

Speed is more important than line.

Jim Flick

If the grass appears shiny, the grain
is growing away from you. The putt will be
faster than it might first appear.

Ken Venturi

The grain has a greater effect late in the day
when the grass is longer.

Nancy Lopez

In the early stages of a long putt, the ball
travels faster and breaks less.

Cary Middlecoff

Look *very* carefully at the area around
the hole. The slower a ball is rolling,
the more it breaks.

Jack Nicklaus

When I am scoring well,
the line of every putt
is as plain to me as if
someone had drawn
it in whitewash.

Bobby Jones

A common fault even among better players
is getting too clever on the greens.

Harvey Penick

Once I have made up my mind as to the line
of a putt and how hard I am going to hit it,
I never change my mind.

Bobby Locke

In putting, decide on some kind of plan —
right or wrong — and stick to it
with confidence.

Curtis Strange

Indecision inevitably erodes confidence.
Have faith in your "read" and go for it.

Arnold Palmer

Never second-guess the line you've selected.
Confusion and doubt are the enemies
of good putting.

Sam Snead

I want to have the total image of the putt's
roll in my mind as I stand over the ball.

Billy Casper

Think of the ball as sitting on a pair of
railroad tracks that run straight into the hole.

Arnold Palmer

Always commit yourself to a specific line
before you set up to the ball.

Lee Trevino

I draw an imaginary line from the ball
to the cup and try to figure the speed needed
to roll along that line.

Gay Brewer

The right speed means hitting a putt
so that the ball that misses the cup finishes
14 to 18 inches past the hole. This distance is
true no matter the length of the putt.

Gary McCord

Once you've judged the speed and line
of a putt, focus on one target and go for it
with confidence.

Ken Venturi

I have one hard and fast rule of putting:
Never hit the ball until you have a good vision
of the path it will roll.

Greg Norman

The art of reading a green can be derived only from experience.

Bobby Jones

We learn to read greens
in the same way that we
learn to read books, by
mastering the basic rules
and then by reading and
reading and reading.

Arnold Palmer

11

The Master's Touch

Once the fundamentals of putting have been mastered, a final challenge remains: the acquisition of "touch." Touch is difficult to define, but we all know it when we see it — or more rarely, when we feel it ourselves.

Lee Trevino noted, "There is no such thing as natural touch. It is something you get from hitting millions of golf balls."

In this chapter, we learn how the world's best golfers acquire the master's touch. The solution seems simple: Read the pages that follow, and don't forget to stroke a few million practice putts.

Judgment of speed and slope count for
very little without the stroke to back it up.

Bobby Jones

In putting, line and touch are everything.

Billy Casper

Putting is strictly a matter of feel, touch
and timing.

Jack Nicklaus

Putting is about those ghostly intangibles —
feel, touch, and nerve —
rather than mechanics.

Gary McCord

How hard do you grip the club when putting?
As lightly as possible.

Ian Woosnam

Putting action must be slow and, above all,
the grip must be loose to maintain
the sensitive touch.

Bobby Locke

People who put a "death grip" on the club
create too much tension. It's impossible
to make a smooth, consistent swing.

Ken Venturi

I don't like the word "grip" because gripping
implies a forceful act, and I don't think that
should be the aim in handling a golf club.

Billy Casper

No one jabs or stabs a putt when the club
is held gently.

Bobby Jones

Hold the putter very loosely.
It can help cure the "jitters."

Bobby Locke

The best putters follow a set routine.
They are what I call pattern putters.
Cary Middlecoff

On short putts, bold is best.
Greg Norman

Firm hitting is the essence of good putting.
Bobby Jones

The thing to remember about putting is that
it is not a power shot.
Billy Casper

People who have an instinctive feel
for what they're doing are going to be better
than people who don't.

Jim Flick

If you're afraid you're going to miss,
you probably will, so forget everything and
concentrate only on getting the ball
into the hole.

Curtis Strange

All that putting requires is a "feel", a touch.

Gay Brewer

Touch largely determines success or failure
on the greens. Touch comes largely
from practice.

Gary Player

Touch can be learned but it can't be taught.

Harvey Penick

12

The Joy of Putting

The two most wonderful sounds in golf are the "click" of a good drive and the brief "tap-tap-tap" of a made putt. But the drive signifies only the beginning of a battle (with much danger ahead), while the putt signifies completion (and hopefully victory).

We conclude with a few thoughts on golf's ultimate stroke. It is not only golf's most important shot, it is also a precursor to golf's most beautiful music. Tap-tap-tap.

Putting greens are to golf courses what faces are to portraits.

Charles Blair Macdonald

Good putting builds and
sustains confidence
all the way around
the golf course.

Gary Player

Nobody putts well every day.

Arnold Palmer

If I made every putt for the rest of my life,
I still wouldn't be even.

Tommy Bolt

There is no tragedy in missing a putt,
no matter how short. All have erred
in this respect.

Walter Hagen

It's not your life, it's not your wife,
it's only a game.

Lloyd Mangrum

I've putted poorly and holed everything. And I've stroked it good and missed everything.

Cary Middlecoff

Even if I'm not hitting the ball very well, I can score well if I'm making my putts.

Tom Watson

When you're putting well, the only question is what part of the hole it's going to fall in, not *if* it's going in.

Jack Nicklaus

When you get the old putter answering, you're hard to beat.

Fuzzy Zoeller

Keep a carefree attitude about your putting.
Do the best you can on every stroke, then
take an accepting attitude toward the results.

Fred Couples

The right of eternal punishment
should be reserved for a higher tribunal than
a greens committee.

Bernard Darwin

Let God's hand rest on your shoulder,
and if it's your turn to win, you will win.

Harvey Penick

I'll tell you why putts go in.
Because the old National Open champion
in the sky puts 'em in.

Bob Rosburg

You can tell a good putt
by the noise it makes.

Bobby Locke

Enjoy the game.
Happy golf is good golf.

Gary Player

Sources

Sources

About Wisdom Books

Wisdom Books chronicle memorable quotations in an easy-to-read style. Written by Criswell Freeman, this series provides inspiring, thoughtful and humorous messages from entertainers, athletes, scientists, politicians, clerics, writers and renegades. Each title focuses on a particular region or area of special interest.

Combining his passion for quotations with extensive training in psychology, Dr. Freeman revisits timeless themes such as perseverance, courage, love, forgiveness and faith.

"Quotations help us remember the simple yet profound truths that give life perspective and meaning," notes Freeman. "When it comes to life's most important lessons, we can all use gentle reminders."

About the Author

Criswell Freeman is a Doctor of Clinical Psychology living in Nashville, Tennessee. He is the author of *When Life Throws You a Curveball, Hit It* and *The Wisdom Series* from WALNUT GROVE PRESS.

The Wisdom Series
by Dr. Criswell Freeman

Regional Titles

Wisdom Made in America	ISBN 1-887655-07-7
The Book of Southern Wisdom	ISBN 0-9640955-3-X
The Wisdom of the Midwest	ISBN 1-887655-17-4
The Wisdom of the West	ISBN 1-887655-31-X
The Book of Texas Wisdom	ISBN 0-9640955-8-0
The Book of Florida Wisdom	ISBN 0-9640955-9-9
The Book of California Wisdom	ISBN 1-887655-14-X
The Book of New York Wisdom	ISBN 1-887655-16-6
The Book of New England Wisdom	ISBN 1-887655-15-8

Sports Titles

The Golfer's Book of Wisdom	ISBN 0-9640955-6-4
The Putter Principle	ISBN 1-887655-39-5
The Golfer's Guide to Life	ISBN 1-887655-38-7
The Wisdom of Southern Football	ISBN 0-9640955-7-2
The Book of Stock Car Wisdom	ISBN 1-887655-12-3
The Wisdom of Old-Time Baseball	ISBN 1-887655-08-5
The Book of Football Wisdom	ISBN 1-887655-18-2
The Book of Basketball Wisdom	ISBN 1-887655-32-8
The Fisherman's Guide to Life	ISBN 1-887655-30-1

Special Interest Titles

The Book of Country Music Wisdom	ISBN 0-9640955-1-3
The Wisdom of Old-Time Television	ISBN 1-887655-64-6
The Wisdom of the Heart	ISBN 1-887655-34-4
The Guide to Better Birthdays	ISBN 1-887655-35-2
The Gardener's Guide to Life	ISBN 1-887655-40-9
Minutes from the Great Women's Coffee Club (by Angela Beasley)	ISBN 1-887655-33-6

Wisdom Books are available through booksellers everywhere.
For information about a retailer near you, call 1-800-256-8584.